STEP-UP
RELIGION

What religions are in our neighbourhood?

Jean Mead

Evans

Published by Evans Brothers Limited
2A Portman Mansions
Chiltern Street
London W1U 6NR

© Evans Brothers Limited 2008

Produced for Evans Brothers Limited by
White-Thomson Publishing Ltd,
Bridgewater Business Centre,
210 High Street,
Lewes, East Sussex BN7 2NH

Printed in China by New Era Printing Co. Ltd.

Project manager: Ruth Nason

Design and illustration: Helen Nelson at
Jet the Dog

British Library Cataloguing in Publication Data

Mead, Jean

What religions are in our neighbourhood? -
(Step-up religion)
1. Religious institutions - Juvenile literature
2. Religions - Juvenile literature
I. Title
200.9

ISBN-13: 9780237534134

Acknowledgements

Many thanks are expressed to Tracey Lockwood
and children at Skyswood School, St Albans, and
Yateen Bhoola and children at Mission Grove
School, Waltham Forest, for their willingness to be
photographed on their visits to places of worship,
and especially for all their work and enthusiasm.
Thanks also for help with this book to Little Heath
Primary School, Potters Bar, and Christ Church,
Little Heath; Camp School, St Albans, and
Abdul-Hakim; St Mary's Church, Marshalswick, and
Revd Chris Davey; Blackhorse Road Baptist Church
and Naaman Murphy; St Albans RE Teachers
Together (SARETT); Ziggie at Sainsburys.

Photographs are from: BAPS Swaminarayan
Sanstha UK: cover tr and page 13r; Chris
Fairclough: cover tl, pages 1/4b, 5t, 7t, 7b, 8b, 11r,
14b, 16, 21t, 24b, 25t, 26, 27t; Jean Mead: cover
(main), pages 4t, 6l, 6r, 8c, 9 (all), 11l, 12 (all),
13l, 14t, 17, 18t, 18cr, 18b, 19t, 19b, 20t, 20b,
22t, 23b, 23t, 24t, 25b, 27b; Michael Nason:
pages 8t, 10, 18cl; Vestry House Museum,
Walthamstow: page 22b; White-Thomson Photo
Library: pages 15l, 15r, 21b (all Chris Fairclough).

Contents

Neighbourhood search

Different neighbourhoods

This book shows how you could investigate the religions that are represented in the neighbourhood around your school. There are many different types of neighbourhoods in the UK. What type of neighbourhood is your school in? For example, is the school in a city, a town or a village?

> Our school is in East London. Especially when we wear our traditional clothes, you can see that our neighbourhood is multicultural.

Neighbourhoods may have different mixtures of people living in them and so there are different religions to investigate depending on where you live and go to school. Some neighbourhoods are multicultural. In other neighbourhoods the people may represent mainly one religion, or perhaps two.

▲ *A neighbourhood is called 'multicultural', when the people there belong to several different races, cultures and religions.*

> Our school is in a district called Marshalswick, on the outskirts of the city of St Albans. Marshalswick has a small shopping centre and several churches.

▶ *A neighbourhood may have more than one place of worship for the same religion. This may be because they belong to different groups, or denominations, in the religion.*

Wherever you are, there are some religions to investigate. In every neighbourhood in England there is likely to be at least one Christian church. The whole of England has been divided into areas called parishes of the Church of England, so everyone has a 'parish church'. These are listed on www.cofe.anglican.org and you can find the name of the parish church for your school.

Starting the search

The first thing to do in your investigation is to search for information about your neighbourhood. Begin by looking at maps of the area around your school. These could be Ordnance Survey maps, local street maps, or maps that you can find online, such as at www.streetmap.co.uk and www.multimap.com.

If you laminate a map of the streets around your school, you can take it with you when you go out to do your investigation and can mark symbols on it.

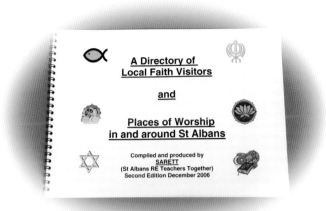

▲ *This directory was made by teachers, to help all schools in their area with their projects to investigate religions.*

To find a list of places of worship in your area, you could look in local telephone directories, or ask at your local library. You may be lucky and find that there is a database or directory of local places of worship, like the one shown above, with information about making contact, but sometimes you and your teacher will need to do the searches yourselves.

▶ *In Ordnance Survey maps a cross symbol is used for for all places of worship, not just churches. Why do you think that is? In some maps different symbols are used for mosques, synagogues, mandirs and gurdwaras.*

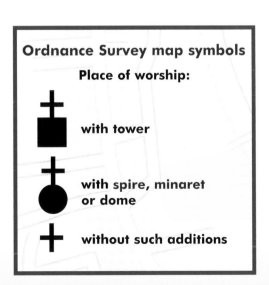

Ordnance Survey map symbols

Place of worship:

with tower

with spire, minaret or dome

without such additions

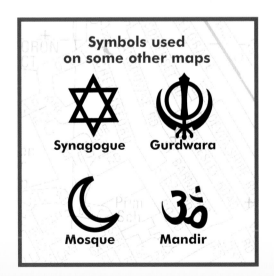

Symbols used on some other maps

Synagogue   **Gurdwara**

Mosque   **Mandir**

Beginning with ourselves

Because you and your class are part of your neighbourhood, it is good to think about yourselves and the groups you belong to. You all belong to the class and the school, but also think about belonging to your family, and to clubs and organisations in the neighbourhood. Some of you may belong to clubs or organisations, such as scouts or guides, that meet in the places of worship you have found on the maps of your neighbourhood.

► *You could make a concept map of 'Groups I belong to', with a picture of you at the centre.*

A map of your life

Make a map of your life in your neighbourhood, putting in your home, school and other places you go to or groups you belong to. What is your favourite place?

Some belong to a religion

Probably the families of some children in your class belong to a religion and go to a place of worship in the neighbourhood. Your teacher may write to your families and ask if anyone would come to give the class an 'insider view' of their religion and place of worship.

▼ *Maybe some people in your class can tell you about their religion. Here, a Muslim boy talks about the Qur'an, the Muslim holy book.*

Me and the groups I belong to

- Badminton club
- Chinese
- Pencil art
- My class: 6B
- Keyboard class
- The Zhang family

Do a survey

How many religions are represented in your class? You will need to think carefully about this, because not everyone can easily answer the question, 'What religion does your family belong to?' There are different ways of 'belonging' to a religion. Some families are very religious and go regularly to their place of worship, but some link with the religion mainly as part of their culture. They may go to the place of worship only for special occasions such as weddings, or at festivals. Some families are not religious at all, so there should be a column on the bar chart for this.

Another way to investigate religions represented in your school is to interview all the people who work there. Make a questionnaire, asking if they belong to a religion and, if so, which religion it is. Include 'I would rather not say' as a possible answer, because some people think this is private.

▶ *Tell the staff you interview for your survey that you will not put any names on display.*

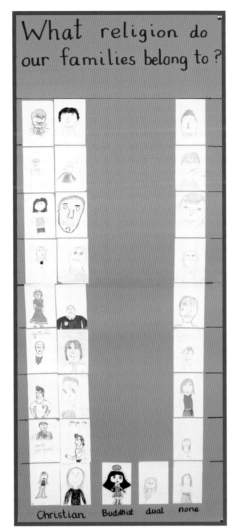

◀ *You could stick pictures of yourselves on a bar chart, like this one made by the class in Marshalswick. Doing this can cause a lot of discussion, and you need to respect what each of you decides to answer.*

▼ *You could use the data from your survey to make pie charts. This one shows the proportion of children from each religion in the class from East London.*

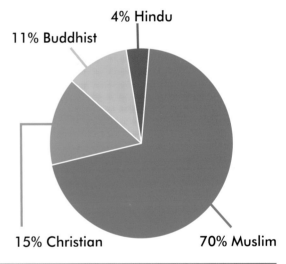

4% Hindu
11% Buddhist
15% Christian
70% Muslim

Walkabout

With a map of your neighbourhood, after you have identified the places of worship, you can plan to go on a walkabout to see what you can find out yourselves about religions in the area. Can you plan a route for the whole class to see all the places of worship, or will you need to separate into smaller groups, each to investigate one or two of the places of worship? Perhaps some parents can be invited to help.

◀ *Places of worship that were specially built, like this church, are easy to recognise. Others may be in houses or other types of buildings and you must look more carefully for them.*

▲ *Plan your route and decide how to*
▶ *record what you find out, and who will use which method. You could take photographs, make video or audio recordings, write notes and draw sketches.*

Buildings where people worship

The most obvious signs of religion in the neighbourhood are the buildings where people go to worship, and these are good places to start your investigations. Pages 10-13 tell you how to recognise different types of places of worship. There may be time on your walkabout to look inside some of the places, and to meet the leaders there. Pages 14-15 give advice about arranging this. But it may be better to fix another time to meet and interview the leader. Even if you just look at a place of worship from the outside, you can still find out quite a lot about it.

Other clues about religions

While out walking, look around for clues about religion in the neighbourhood, in or on:

- people, their clothes or badges
- symbols or stickers on cars
- houses: for example, posters in windows, signs over doors, little boxes on the doorposts of Jewish homes, called mezuzahs
- shops

◀▼ What can you tell about religions from these three clues?

- cemeteries, almshouses or places connected with charities
- names of schools: many schools were started by churches or other groups of religious people, and are linked to them
- street names: these may give clues about religion in the past. Some may be easy to recognise, such as Church Road, but others may include names like Chapel, Priory, Mission and Glebelands, which you may need to look up in a dictionary
- buildings that have changed from one use to another: these may be clues to religion in the past (Also see pages 22-23.)

▲ *There may be religious bookshops or food shops (for example, selling halal food, which is Muslim, or kosher food, which is Jewish). Jewellery and card shops might have religious items on display.*

Make a display

Make a display of photographs, sketches or descriptions to show all the clues you discovered about religion around your neighbourhood.

Types of church building

There are many different types of Christian churches, and you can find out about the ones in your neighbourhood. From their name, usually on the notice board outside, you can find which denomination of the Christian religion they belong to.

Church of England churches

Often the oldest religious building in a neighbourhood is a parish church belonging to the Church of England. This Christian denomination began at the time of the Reformation in the sixteenth century, when Protestant and Roman Catholic Christianity separated, but some Church of England buildings are older than that.

How old is the Church of England church in your neighbourhood? Not all of them are old, but many are.

▲ Some parish churches have a tower, or a spire with a cross on top. The windows are often made of stained glass and have a pointed shape. Some churches have a graveyard around them.

Understanding the architecture

Ask your local vicar or minister (or both) to come and tell you about their church and especially to explain the function of various parts of the building and the beliefs they represent.

▲ *Many Roman Catholic churches have a crucifix outside.*

Roman Catholic churches

You can often identify a Roman Catholic church from its statues of saints or from a cross with a figure of Jesus on it, called a crucifix. Some Roman Catholic churches have a rounded end called an apse.

Orthodox churches

Where lots of Greek people live, there may be Greek Orthodox churches. In some places in the UK, people from this denomination have converted other church buildings, which were no longer used, to make them suitable for Greek Orthodox worship.

Non-conformist churches

Non-conformist denominations include Baptists, Methodists, United Reformed, Evangelical, Pentecostal, Brethren, Salvation Army and Society of Friends (Quakers). Some of their buildings are called chapels or meeting rooms, instead of churches. Some look plain and simple, because the people want to worship God without the distraction of images. In your neighbourhood, what clues are there, from the outside, that these buildings are Christian places of worship?

▶ *Non-conformist (also called 'free') churches are built in many styles but are usually designed for people to sit and listen, as listening to teaching from the Bible is a main part of their worship.*

Newer groups

You may find buildings used by groups such as Jehovah's Witnesses, Mormons and Seventh Day Adventists. These groups were linked to Christianity, but some of their beliefs are different from most Christian teaching.

Other places of worship

In some neighbourhoods there are places of worship for other religions, as well as Christian churches. Even if your neighbourhood does not have any of these, it is interesting to know about them, and you will be able to recognise them when you visit other places.

Some buildings used as places of worship were something else before, such as houses, church halls, or shops. These may not look like places of worship outside, or they may have been changed and redecorated in a suitable style. Other places of worship have been purpose-built by people from the religion, usually in the design that is traditional for that religion.

Masjid - e - Umer

▲ The traditional features of a mosque, the Muslim place of worship, are a dome and towers called minarets. This follows a design that the Prophet Muhammad began in Arabia, in the 7th century. 'Masjid' is the Arabic name for a mosque. What symbol of Islam can you see on this mosque?

▶ Many religions have a symbol that identifies them, and it may be used to show their places of worship. A wheel with eight spokes is a symbol of Buddhism.

◀ A gurdwara is the Sikh place of worship. There is always a flag, called the Nishan Sahib, outside a gurdwara. It is triangular and saffron-coloured and has the khanda symbol on it. The tall flag-pole is wrapped in saffron-coloured cloth.

▲ The design of a *menorah* symbol on this synagogue gate shows that the building is Jewish. Another Jewish symbol you may see is the *star of David*. The name on a synagogue may say which branch of Judaism it belongs to, such as Orthodox, Reform or Liberal.

Times to visit

Many places of worship also act as community centres, holding language classes and social activities for people from a particular country. The buildings may be open during the week for prayers or community activities.

At a mosque, there are five short prayer times every day, but the main prayer time is at Friday lunchtime, and so Fridays are not a good time for a school visit to a mosque. Friday afternoons are also not a good time for a school party to visit a synagogue, as the Jewish Sabbath or holy day begins at Friday sunset. Sikhs and Hindus do not have a special holy day each week, but often their main meetings are at weekends.

▼ Some Hindu places of worship are called temples and some are called mandirs (the Hindu word for 'temples'). Many are named for one or more of the Hindu deities that are worshipped there, and an 'om' symbol (right) identifies the building as Hindu. There are few purpose-built Hindu temples in Britain, but this famous and beautiful one at Neasden in London is built in a traditional Indian style, from white marble.

Go on a virtual tour

Choose one type of place of worship that interests you, go to www.reonline.org.uk/juniors >virtual tours, and choose a building to explore online.

Making contact and showing respect

Your class may be divided into groups, each to investigate a different place of worship in the neighbourhood. With your teacher's help, your group will need to make contact with someone at the place of worship, to arrange to meet him or her.

At some places of worship, the best person to speak to is the leader, but at others there may be someone different to help you. There may be someone who is more used to talking to children. If your group can visit the place of worship to interview the person, you can also see inside the building to learn about it.

▶ *If you wish to contact someone at a place of worship by phone, try to be patient and allow time for the person to call back, because he or she may be very busy with other things. There is not always someone available all the time. It might be good to email the person, if you have an address.*

Alternatively, the leader or other representative of a place of worship might come to your school to answer your questions.

▼ *Abdul-Hakim is the Education Officer for a mosque and enjoys talking to children from local schools.*

Showing respect

You will want to be polite and show respect, so try to find out the way to behave with the people you will meet in the place of worship. This may be different in different cultures. You can ask:

- What would you like us to call you? There may be a title to use, such as 'Father [and a first name]' for a Roman Catholic priest, or 'Rabbi' for a Jewish rabbi.

- Is there a polite way to greet people? It might be a handshake. If you go to a mosque, people will say, 'A salaam wa leikum' (peace be upon you), to which you can reply, 'Wa leikum a salaam' (and peace be upon you too).

▶ At a mandir people greet each other by saying 'Namaste' and making a little bow, with hands held together.

Different places, different behaviour

Think of two places you have visited (for example, your grandparents' home, a swimming pool, a school, a place of worship, a concert hall) and write a list for each of how you dress, speak and behave there. Why are there differences?

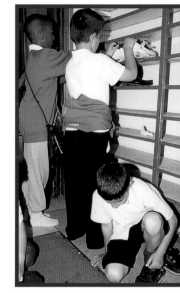

▶ In many cultures people don't wear shoes indoors, so in mosques, gurdwaras and mandirs you should expect to take your shoes off. (So wear clean socks!)

- Are there rules about what to wear? Jewish, Muslim and Sikh men and boys wear head coverings in their places of worship, so find out if boys going to visit a synagogue, mosque or gurdwara should do the same. At mosques and gurdwaras, girl visitors will be asked to cover their heads with a scarf. For visiting a place of worship where you will be expected to sit on the floor, it is probably best if girls wear trousers.

- Are there particular rules about respectful behaviour? Must visitors follow these? For example, in a gurdwara, worshippers bow down in front of the holy book, the Guru Granth Sahib, but it is usually all right for visitors just to stand respectfully in front of it when they enter. It is disrespectful to turn your back on, or to sit with feet facing, the Guru Granth Sahib, or the front in a mosque.

- Is it all right to take photographs?

- Are there things that you must not touch?

Group work and questionnaires

There are many ways to investigate a place of worship. You can be like 'detectives', looking carefully at the building for clues and interviewing people to find answers to your questions. You can also collect information about the religion to which the place of worship belongs by researching in books and on the internet. When you undertake this task as a group, you are a 'community of learning', working together, sharing your knowledge and skills and the effort of finding out. What do you like about working in this type of group?

A know/want/learnt table

A good way to organise your group learning and to record your work is a 'know, want, learnt (KWL) table'. This has three columns.

What we already know	What we want to know	What we have learnt

- In the first column, record what anyone in the group already knows about the place of worship and the religion to which it belongs. Write down what you think you know, even if you are unsure, as you can check it out in your investigation.

▲ *In the 'What we want to know' column use the questioning words, Who?, Why?, What? Where?, When? and How? as headings.*

- In the second column, list what you want to know: for example, about the person you are going to interview at the place of worship; the people who use the building; the building itself; and the religion. Think about questions that will help you to understand what is important.

- The third column is for you to record all that you have learnt, at the end of your investigation. How much room do you think you will need to leave for this?

Write and use a questionnaire

In your group, use the first two columns of your KWL table to help you to write a questionnaire. Each of you should think about what interests or puzzles you and make a list of five questions that you would ask the person you are going to interview at the place of worship. Then compare your lists and choose ten questions that you all agree are important.

Write out the ten questions clearly, make a copy each, and make one copy with spaces for writing in the answers that the person gives. Decide who will ask each question, and who will write down the answer. Try to arrange to take a photo of your group doing the interview, for when you present your findings.

You could also use your questionnaire to interview someone at school from the religion you are researching. You might hear some different answers, because people don't all understand their religion in the same way.

Trying out questions

Good questionnaires have a mixture of closed questions, which can be answered 'yes' or 'no', and open questions inviting a longer answer. From your 'want' column, make up two of each kind of question and try them out in your group.

▼ *It can be quite scary to interview someone you don't know, but if you have thought of good questions to ask, you will be less nervous. It will also mean that you won't waste time. If it is not possible to arrange an interview, you could perhaps send your questionnaire to the person at the place of worship.*

Baptist Church Questionnaire
Person interviewed _____

Questions and answers	Who will ask and who will write?
1 How long has the church been here?	Kiani Levi
2 What is the difference between a Baptist church and the Church of England?	Zainab Yasmin
3 How many people come here?	Levi Kiani
...en they come to church?	Yasmin

Evidence from notice boards and empty buildings

Usually when you visit places of worship during school days, the buildings are empty. It can be difficult to imagine what the places are like when they are in use by the people who worship there. You will need to use some detective work and your imaginations to help your investigation, asking questions about what you see.

▶ *A name board usually shows the religion, or branch of a religion, to which a place of worship belongs. Some boards include other information, such as the name of the religious leader or secretary, a phone number, and the times of the main meetings for worship. At churches, these are called services.*

◀ *In the entrance hall of many places of worship there are notice boards from which you can find out what happens there, what types of groups of people go there, what the people who go there are interested in, and how they care for others.*

Make a note of what can be learnt from the outside of the building you are investigating (see pages 10-13). From the outside of the building, and from its entrance hall, do you have the feeling that it is a friendly place that people like to come to?

▲ When you go into the worship hall of a mandir, you will see the main shrine, with statues of the Hindu deities.

The centre of attention

When you first go into the main worship or prayer room, notice what is at the centre at the front: for example, an altar, where a service called communion happens; a place for the holy book; or a place for the prayer leader. What you see is a big clue to what is most important for people in the religion.

Pictures and symbols

Look around the room to see whether it is plain or decorated, or has pictures or statues. There are differing ideas about whether it is right or wrong to have pictures in a place of worship. Can you find out why the place of worship you are investigating looks as it does? If there are pictures, what are they about? Are there symbols you can draw and find out their meaning?

What is it like for worshippers?

Some people you meet at the place of worship may be willing to read out a short passage from their holy book, or tell you what worship means to them. Some places of worship are used for prayers during the day, so find out if people mind you watching. You may be able instead to see a video or pictures of people worshipping in that religion.

► Ask questions on your visit, to try to find out what the place feels like when people worship there.

Pictures and labels

Make sketches, take photographs and write notes about what you see. Choose one thing to research further, so that you can write a label about what it is and what it means. You can use this later in a display.

Finding out about key beliefs

Investigating is not just describing what you see, but also trying to understand it. To understand a religion, we need to know more than what people from the religion do; we need to know why they do it. The 'Why?' questions in the 'Want' column of your KWL table (see page 16) are very important.

People who belong to a religion are called 'believers', and the things they believe influence what they do. The most important beliefs of a religion are called its 'key beliefs'. Understanding them is like a key that will open the way to understanding everything in the religion. Key beliefs are likely to be about:

- God

- how to know God

- the holy book

- how to worship

- how God wants people to behave.

Notice which things seem important in a place of worship and this will help you to find out about the people's key beliefs.

▼ *In a church you will probably notice the cross symbol. The cross seems very important to Christians. If you ask about this, you will be told that it is a symbol of the death of Jesus on a cross, like the crucifix on page 11. An empty cross shows the belief that Jesus did not stay dead but came back to life again.*

◄ *You could look at hymn books in a church, as part of investigating Christian beliefs. You could look for hymns that mention the cross.*

How did we find out?

Write out two key beliefs that you have learnt about in the religion you are investigating, and discuss with your group how you discovered them. Were there clues in what you saw or heard, or read or found on a website?

Some books and websites are written for people who belong to the religion. Some are written to explain the beliefs to others. What difference does this make to how easy they are to understand, or how interesting they are?

Beliefs about God

Beliefs about God are quite hard to understand. For example, in a mandir you will see many gods and goddesses, but you may find out that many Hindus believe that these all show different aspects of only one God.

Some religions have a statement that sums up their key beliefs. For example, in Islam, there is the Shahadah, a declaration that 'There is no god except Allah, and Muhammad is the Messenger of Allah'. This shows that Muslims do not believe Muhammad to be God in the way that Christians believe about Jesus. Sikhism and Christianity have creeds, which are lists of key beliefs.

Beliefs about holy books

In some religions, the holy book is believed to be the 'Word of God'. Understanding this will help you to understand why the books are treated with love and respect in places of worship.

▼ *The most important Jewish holy book is the Torah. In a synagogue, the Torah scrolls, dressed in 'mantles', are kept in the Ark.*

Linking with history

In the 'Want' column of your KWL table (see page 16), you may have questions such as 'When was the place of worship built?' or 'When did it become a place of worship?' The answers you find can also be clues to the history of your neighbourhood.

How old is the place of worship you are investigating? Has the building always been used in the same way, or have there been changes? To find answers, you could ask the person you interview at the place of worship, or there may be a leaflet giving information. The style of the building is a clue to when it was built, and sometimes a foundation stone can help you.

◀ This foundation stone was laid when a new hall was added to a synagogue building. At the top is some writing in *Hebrew*.

▲ The rabbi (right) and the Berry family held a foundation stone ceremony. Perhaps you can visit a local museum and find old maps and photographs like this of your neighbourhood, to compare with what you have seen.

Oral history

See if you can meet some older people who have lived in your neighbourhood a long time. Show them your walkabout map and pictures and tell them what you have learnt. Ask them what religion in the neighbourhood was like when they were young.

Changes in your neighbourhood

Your neighbourhood hasn't always been the same as now. The population has changed at times, for many reasons. Places of worship were built, changed or demolished to meet the needs of the changing population. In Victorian times, when large numbers of people moved from the country to the towns and cities, many Non-conformist churches were built (the one on page 8 is an example), and many Roman Catholic churches were built for Irish people who moved to England to find work.

As various groups of people have settled in Britain, they have tended to stay together and make certain areas their home. Here they have needed their own places of worship. At first they may have used houses or unwanted church buildings. Later they may have been able to build new places of worship that show their own traditions and style.

▼ *This building in Brick Lane, East London, is an interesting example of change. It was built as a Protestant chapel, by Huguenots who had fled from persecution in France. Later, Jewish people moved into the area and the building was changed into a synagogue. Later still, Bangladeshi people arrived and the building became a mosque.*

In the mid-20th century many black immigrants came from the Caribbean. Some were Christians but they felt unwelcomed by churches in Britain, and so they started new, black-led churches, to worship in their own ways.

▼ *These people from different races all worship at the same church, but there are also separate churches for people from different backgrounds. Can you say why?*

▼ *Place names can give clues about religion in the past. Eccles is from the Latin word 'Ecclesia' for church. Saxon churches linked to monasteries were called 'minsters'. Kirk is the Viking name for church.*

23

Presenting your findings

When you have finished your investigation about the place of worship, it is time to put together everything that you have found out. You can look back at the questions you wrote on your 'Know/Want/Learnt' table (page 16), and see if you have discovered all that you wished. In the 'Learnt' column, you can now record all the knowledge and understanding you have gained in your investigations.

It might be that there is a lot of information but it is all rather muddled, because you have gathered evidence from different parts of your investigation. Your group now needs to sort the information in a way that will make sense when you present it to others in your class.

▲ *You need to decide which are the most important and interesting things to report about the place of worship you investigated.*

◀ *How does it feel to have completed your investigation?*

I never knew there was so much to find out about our neighbourhood! It's been really interesting investigating the church down the road and learning what it's all about.

You could write each piece of information on a post-it note, and then all try to put these pieces into sets of things that go together. Next match the sets of information to the evidence you have found, such as photos, sketches and notes about the building; objects you have been able to borrow; photos and notes of your interview; book pages and extracts from the internet. An interesting way to do this is to arrange everything on a table to make a 'concept map' of your learning. Then, to present your work to

What colour background would be suitable for your presentation? Green was chosen for this 'concept map', as this was the colour of the altar cloth and vestments that the children saw at the church they investigated.

the rest of the class, you might ask everyone to stand around your table, while you present the 'map' to them and explain the items in it. Another way would be to use the interactive whiteboard.

Let people ask questions and tell you what they thought about your presentation. There might be things that people did not understand at first and you can explain more clearly. Make a note of any changes you would like to make, and use this to edit and improve your presentation. You might need to cut out some less important material if there is too much. When it is another group's turn to present their findings, listen carefully and ask questions about anything you don't understand.

Thank you letter
Write a thank you letter to the person you met at the place of worship, saying what you learned from your investigation and why it was worthwhile.

The end of the project

At the end of your project the whole class could make a 'religious trail', put their findings into a display, or do an assembly to show the school. It would be very useful to make a directory of information about local places of worship, or an illustrated book of the religious trail, for others to use. Could you invite everyone who has helped or been interviewed in the investigation to see the final result?

▼ *Make a religious trail by linking pictures and information to a route on a map.*

Similarities and differences

As a class you can now start to compare the places of worship you have investigated. You could make a grid to list the similarities and differences between them. For example, two places of worship may both have a holy book, but treat it in different ways.

Comparing different churches

If all the places of worship in your neighbourhood belong to Christianity, it is interesting to compare:

- their attitudes towards the Bible
- their beliefs about communion
- what their worship services are like
- what the buildings look like and why
- when people are baptised and how.

The similarities you notice are likely to be in the 'key beliefs' of Christianity, although you might find some differences in beliefs between Christian denominations.

If you belong to a church school, have you been able to learn about a denomination or religion that is different from the school's?

▲ *In your class there will probably be some different opinions, as you are dealing with questions that many people disagree about. It will be great if you can respect each other's opinions, knowing that you have all worked hard to understand the things you have been learning about.*

Comparing different religions

If your neighbourhood has places of worship of different religions, it is interesting to discuss how their key beliefs are different, as well as the look of their buildings and the way the people do things. Are there some things that all the religions agree about?

Considering what you have learnt

Has your investigation helped you to understand more about people from different religions in your class or neighbourhood?

If you belong to a religion yourself, has doing this investigation helped you to understand your own religion better, and made you more able to help others understand it?

When you go to new places now, you can use the skills you have gained in this investigation. Look for clues about religion (see page 9), and try to recognise different places of worship (pages 10-13). If you meet people from religions you have investigated, you can talk to them about what you have learnt, and maybe go on learning more from them.

What skills and understanding do you think Emily and Baris gained from investigating the religions in their neighbourhoods?

I really liked working with my group. It was fun to share the work and sort out how to find out things together. Although some of us are Christians and some aren't, we all learned new things.

I am a Muslim and I talked to the minister at the church and found out what Christians really believe about Jesus. I told him we call Jesus Isa and he is one of the prophets in the Qur'an too.

Comparing neighbourhoods

It could be interesting for you to link with a school in a different sort of neighbourhood and tell each other about your investigations. It might be possible to email them to talk about your findings or send each other some of your work.

27

Glossary

almshouses   houses for the poor or elderly paid for out of the alms (gifts) of Christians or other charity.

altar   a wood or stone table where offerings are made to God. In a church, the altar is where the bread and wine are prepared. Some denominations refer to it as the communion table.

apse   a semicircular part at the east end of some churches, containing the altar.

Ark   in a synagogue, the cupboard in which the Torah scrolls are kept.

baptise   to welcome into the Christian religion by a ceremony involving immersion in, or pouring or sprinkling of, water.

cemetery   an area of ground in which the dead are buried.

chapel   a Non-conformist place of worship, or a prayer area in a church/building.

Church of England   the official church in England, ruled by bishops and with the Queen as its head. Church of England churches are also called Anglican churches.

communion   a Christian service with bread and wine, which recalls the last meal of Jesus and celebrates his sacrificial death. Also called Holy Communion, Eucharist, Mass, Lord's Supper.

creed   a summary statement of religious beliefs, often recited in worship.

crucifix   a model or image of Jesus dying on a cross.

culture   background of ideas and values held by a particular group of people.

deities   gods and goddesses.

denominations   religious groups: for example, in Christianity, Roman Catholic, Church of England, Baptists and Methodists.

foundation stone   a stone with a date and sometimes other information, put in to mark the start of a building.

glebelands   farm lands given to the church to provide income for the clergy.

Greek Orthodox   the Greek Church holding the Eastern Orthodox faith, which separated from western Christianity in 1054.

gurdwara   a Sikh place of worship or temple.

halal   in Islam, approved or allowed by the Qur'an or the Prophet Muhammad.

Hebrew   Jewish language. The Jewish holy book is written in Hebrew.

Huguenots   French Protestants in the 16th-17th century who were cruelly persecuted in France. Many escaped to England.

hymn   a song of praise, especially to God.

khanda   the Sikh symbol; and also the double-edged sword in the centre of it.

kosher   a Jewish word for 'fit' or 'proper'; permitted by Jewish laws.

mandir   a Hindu temple or place of worship.

mantle   a cover, like a cloak, for a Torah scroll.

menorah	a seven-branched candlestick which was lit daily in the Jewish Temple in Jerusalem and has become a symbol for Judaism.
mezuzah	a small scroll in a decorative box, fixed to a Jewish doorpost. The scroll contains a section of the Torah.
minaret	a tall slender tower attached to a mosque, from which, in Muslim countries, the call to prayer is made.
minister	a member of the clergy, or leader in a Non-conformist church. Some churches use the word 'pastor'.
mission	a church that is supported by a larger church or organisation, for telling a community about the Christian faith.
monastery	a building where a group of monks live and work.
mosque	a Muslim place of worship.
multicultural	containing people from several different cultures or ethnic groups.
Namaste	the Hindu word and gesture of greeting and farewell, which originally meant, 'I salute the god within you'.
Non-conformist	Protestant churches in England other than the Church of England. They are also called 'free churches' as they are not ruled by the Church of England.
om	the sacred syllable chanted in Hindu prayers.
parish	an area of the country as divided up by the Church of England or the Roman Catholic Church.
priory	a monastery or convent headed by a prior or prioress.

Protestant	the branch of western Christianity that separated from Roman Catholicism in the 16th century, and believes that the Bible is the ultimate authority for Christians.
rabbi	the religious leader of a Jewish community. It means 'my teacher'.
Reformation	a 16th-century reform movement which led to the formation of Protestant Churches. It emphasised the need to return to the beliefs and practices of the early Church.
Roman Catholic	Christian denomination that regards the Pope as head of the Church.
Sabbath	a holy day each week, set apart for rest from work.
saint	a particularly good or holy person; usually someone believed to have gone to heaven after their death.
service	a religious worship meeting or ceremony.
Shahadah	the Muslim declaration of faith.
spire	a tall, thin, cone-shaped structure on top of a building.
star of David	a symbol of the Jewish faith, a six-pointed star.
synagogue	a Jewish place of worship and community centre.
Torah	the most important Jewish holy book consisting of the first five books of the Bible.
vestments	robes worn by leaders during a religious ceremony.
vicar	a priest in the Church of England.

For teachers and parents

This book has been designed to support and extend the learning objectives of Unit 4D of the QCA Religious Education Scheme of Work, 'What religions are represented in our neighbourhood?' It is a generic RE theme, encouraging children to investigate the school neighbourhood whether that is a country village, an inner city or anything in-between. The book features children from two contrasting schools as they go through the processes of investigating their very different neighbourhoods, and provides guidance and a supportive framework for pupils as they explore, develop enquiry skills and understanding of key beliefs, and present and evaluate their findings. It would be helpful also for the 2006 QCA Year 5 Unit, 'What do places of worship teach us about religions?'

The content and suggested activities aim to help children to learn both 'about religion' (AT1) and 'from religion' (AT2), as identified in the Non-Statutory Framework KS2; and especially to fulfil the requirement that they learn from 'a religious community with a significant local presence'(3c). It should help children to develop self-awareness, respect for all and open-mindedness, which are important attitudes in Religious Education, as well as children's personal, social, cultural and moral education.

FURTHER INFORMATION AND ACTIVITIES

Pages 4-5 Neighbourhood search

Teachers will need to do prior investigations, risk assessment and setting up preliminary contacts, in order for children to be able to explore safely and effectively, but should aim that the children achieve as great a sense of ownership of the investigation as possible.

Letters home at the outset, emphasising the educational aim of understanding, will help to obtain parental consent for the visits, but you will need to take any parental right of withdrawal from RE into account, and may need to allocate some children to investigating religions acceptable to their parents.

The local Standing Advisory Council for Religious Education (SACRE) or LEA Advisory Service may have information or a database about contacts with places of worship in the area.

Find and compare different maps of the neighbourhood and discuss maps for different purposes, as a link to Geography.

The Church of England website www.cofe.anglican.org/links/dios.html can be used to locate parish churches, but navigating it varies according to your diocese. A non-denominational church-finding site is www.findachurch.co.uk. Some links are very informative but it is not an exhaustive list.

Pages 6-7 Beginning with ourselves

Help children to reflect on groups they belong to. In pairs they can think about what they gain from being part of a community, about commitment (loyalty) and why people of the same religion might want to meet regularly.

Give children the opportunity to talk about religious groups they and their families belong to, but be sensitive to reluctance, and ensure that everybody is treated with respect. If children or parents volunteer to be questioned about their religion, be clear that you value their insider views without necessarily expecting them to know everything.

Link with Maths in finding ways of recording data you collect about religions represented in the school. Note the sensitivities needed when asking about religion and discuss the range of meaning of belonging.

Discuss the differences between the two charts shown, and why staff data may not be the same as class data for a neighbourhood.

Pages 8-9 Walkabout

Ask the children to be 'detectives' looking for clues about religion on their routes to school, and stick evidence around a map of the neighbourhood with your walkabout findings.

On a range of maps, see how many street names you can find with possible religious connections and make a display of street signs with dictionary definitions. This might link to the local history pages 22-23.

Pages 10-11 Types of church building

Link to History topics such as the Tudors. Explore the religious reasons for the Reformation, to help children understand the reasons for the changes in church buildings and practices. Discuss how events can be seen from two different perspectives.

Find church booklets or local history books to identify the period of building or altering of your local church. *Faith in History* by Margaret Cooling has strong links to the History NC. Reference books such as Stephen Friar's *A Companion to the English Parish Church* can be useful. Also see www.request.org.uk/main/history.

Link to Geography: use a compass to check the orientation of your local Anglican churches. They usually face east, towards Jerusalem.

Websites for denominations usually give their history and key beliefs.

If there are buildings of 'para-Christian sects', you can investigate how their beliefs and practices differ from mainstream Christianity.

In cities, cathedrals are usually open every day and many have an education service for school visits, and their own websites.

Pages 12-13 Other places of worship

As well as the site mentioned in the activity box there are other virtual visits online such as on your local 'grid for learning'.

If your local example of a place of worship for a religion is in an adapted building which does not provide a good presentation of the traditional style, try to find attractive examples in books or online.

The Neasden mandir is the largest outside India. See www.mandir.org.

Buddhist temples have not been included as they are rare in the UK. The Buddhist Society (0208 7834 5858) will tell you if there is a monastery or centre near you. Some virtual tours are on REonline.

Pages 14-15 Making contact and showing respect

A preliminary session on children's own special places, talking about how they would like guests to behave there, can help to motivate pupils to behave with respect in other people's special places.

When you make initial contact, try to ensure tactfully that the person to be interviewed has clear enough English to be understood by the children, and is able to speak to non-members without evangelising. The National Association of Teachers of RE has a helpful leaflet called 'Religious believers visiting schools': see www.natre.org.uk.

Try not to be intimidated by unfamiliar religions or cultures. A respectful attitude and willingness to learn are what are important, and people at places of worship are usually happy to explain about expectations of dress and behaviour.

Ask hosts at places of worship not to require visitors from other religions to do anything that would offend. Some Muslim, Jewish and Christian families would find bowing to images, or the Guru Granth Sahib, unacceptable. Eating food that has been offered in worship in Hindu temples can be an issue, but this can be resolved with courtesy.

Pages 16-17 Group work and questionnaires

This project can be an opportunity to foster thinking skills and encourage children to take control of their own learning.

A useful strategy when writing questionnaires is to ask children to suggest three sensible and three silly/unsuitable questions each, pool them and as a group identify and discard the unsuitable ones.

Pages 18-19 Evidence from notice boards and empty buildings

When a group goes into an empty place of worship, give children the opportunity to sit separately and quietly for a few minutes to become aware of the atmosphere and how it makes them feel. Discussing different perceptions can be productive as long as it is not intruding on children's privacy.

Religions' attitudes towards buildings may vary, some regarding the building as 'holy' and some believing that God is present in the people rather than in the building as such.

Pages 20-21 Finding out about key beliefs

Websites of some places of worship, denominations and religions have sections on key beliefs. While it is a useful skill for pupils to be able to handle authentic material written for use within a religion, some 'vetting' of web browsing may be needed.

Pages 22-23 Linking with history

There may be links with periods of history the children are studying: Saxon crosses or parts of church buildings; Viking 'stave' or wooden churches (these rarely survive but possibly the oldest existing wooden church is at Greensted in Essex); Tudor and Stuart churches reflecting the great religious changes of the period; churches built in the Victorian era; rebuilding and changes since 1948 (population changes have brought peoples from across the world and their religions, although these may be concentrated in particular areas).

Tower Hamlets www.movinghere.org.uk >schools>people and places>changing landscapes has an interactive map of changes in Brick Lane among interesting material and teaching ideas for history.

www.request.org.uk/main/churches >African and Caribbean has pictures and an account of worship in an Afro-Caribbean church.

Look out for and investigate any buildings in your neighbourhood which have a different use from the one they were originally built for.

Pages 24-25 Presenting your findings

Organising, evaluating and presenting the evidence provides an excellent cross-curricular opportunity to contribute to the Literacy Strategy target T27 of making a non-chronological report.

Pages 26-27 Similarities and differences

Mainstream churches are likely to have key beliefs about God and Jesus in common, but sects such as Jehovah's Witnesses differ.

Comparing religions can be problematic as there is rarely an exact equivalence between them. It is usually best to look for an underlying concept that is expressed in the respective religions rather than saying that beliefs and practices are the same.

Consider extending the work by organising an internet exchange with a school in a different area, to compare and analyse differences.

USEFUL WEBSITES

www.qca.org.uk >I am interested in>Subjects>Religious Education> Useful resources

www.reonline.org.uk is a 'gateway' RE site. It has a child-friendly junior section, including virtual visits to places of worship.

www.request.org.uk is an excellent site for a wide range of work on Christianity and links to different types of churches.

www.re-xs.ucsm.ac.uk is another useful 'gateway' site.

Index